WITHDRAWN

Swimming Science

Hélène Boudreau

Crabtree Publishing Company

www.crabtreebooks.com

Crabtree Publishing Company

www.crabtreebooks.com

Author: Hélène Boudreau

Editors: Molly Aloian
Leon Gray

Proofreaders: Adrianna Morganelli
Crystal Sikkens

Project coordinator: Robert Walker

Production coordinator: Margaret Amy Salter

Prepress technician: Margaret Amy Salter

Designer: Lynne Lennon

Picture researcher: Sean Hannaway

Managing editor: Tim Cooke

Art director: Jeni Child

Design manager: David Poole

Editorial director: Lindsey Lowe

Children's publisher: Anne O'Daly

Photographs:

Action Images: Paulo Santos: page 5 (top); Christophe Launay: page 5 (bottom); CSPA: pages 6–7; Jim Young: page 9 (top); Christinne Muschi: pages 14–15, 21 (top), 24–25; Stephane Kempinaire: pages 15, 18, 19 (bottom left and right); Vincent Kessler: page 17 (top); Brent Smith: page 19 (top); David Callow: page 20; MDB: page 21 (bottom); Gustau Nacarino: page 22; Wolfgang Rattay: page 23 (top); Philippe Millereau: page 23 (bottom); Jeff Haynes: page 25 (top); Nigel Roddis: page 25 (bottom); Kimimasa Mayama: page 26; Sporting Pictures: page 27 (bottom)

Ansys Inc: page 29 (bottom)

Corbis: Bettmann: page 13 (bottom); Ted Levine: page 16

Getty Images: Al Bello: page 4; Timothy A. Clary: page 7 (top); Martin Bernetti: page 7 (bottom); Daniel Berehulak: page 8; Quinn Rooney: page 10; Jose Luis Roca: page 11 (top left); Greg Wood: pages 12–13; Donald Miralle: page 14; Adam Pretty: page 27 (top)

PA Photos: Anders Wiklund: page 17 (bottom); Chris Ison: page 28; Luis M. Alvarez: page 29 (top)

Shutterstock: Vasily Smirnov: front cover; Gert Johannes Jacobus Vrey: backgrounds; Yana Petruseva: page 11 (center left); AGphotographer: page 11 (center left); Regien Paassen: page 11 (center left); Filip Fuxa: page 11 (center left)

Illustrations:

Mark Walker: page 12

Every effort has been made to trace the owners of copyrighted material.

Library and Archives Canada Cataloguing in Publication

Boudreau, Hélène, 1969-
 Swimming science / Hélène Boudreau.

(Sports science)
Includes index.
ISBN 978-0-7787-4538-9 (bound).--ISBN 978-0-7787-4555-6 (pbk.)

 1. Swimming--Juvenile literature. 2. Sports sciences--Juvenile literature. I. Title. II. Series: Sports science (St. Catharines, Ont.)

GV837.6.B69 2008   j797.2'1015   C2008-907433-5

Library of Congress Cataloging-in-Publication Data

Boudreau, Hélène.
 Swimming science / Hélène Boudreau.
  p. cm. -- (Sports science)
 Includes index.
 ISBN 978-0-7787-4555-6 (pbk. : alk. paper) -- ISBN 978-0-7787-4538-9 (reinforced library binding : alk. paper)
 1. Swimming--Juvenile literature. 2. Sports Sciences--Juvenile literature. I. Title. II. Series.

GV837.6.B68 2009
797.2'1--dc22

2008048870

Crabtree Publishing Company

www.crabtreebooks.com   1-800-387-7650

Published in Canada
Crabtree Publishing
616 Welland Ave.
St. Catharines, Ontario
L2M 5V6

Published in the United States
Crabtree Publishing
PMB16A
350 Fifth Ave., Suite 3308
New York, NY 10118

Contents

Introducing Swimming

Cave paintings from more than 6,000 years ago show that people have been swimming since prehistoric times. Through the ages, people swam to travel across bays, lakes, and rivers. They also swam to fish for food and for fun.

Swimming as a sport began in England in the 1800s. Competitive swimming appeared at the first modern Olympic Games in Athens in 1896. Swimmers were dropped into the icy waters of the Mediterranean Sea.

Outdoor pools are popular in places where the climate is hot and dry.

▶▶▶▶▶▶▶▶▶

FACT!

Different strokes

FINA has approved four strokes for competitive swimming races. They are the front crawl (or freestyle), breaststroke, backstroke, and butterfly.

NEW WORDS

FINA: The Fédération Internationale de Natation is the world governing body for swimming competitions.

LOOK CLOSER

Amazon Swim 2007

Martin Strel of Slovenia (pictured right) was tired on April 7, 2007. That day he finished his 3,270-mile (5,268-km) swim along the Amazon River—the longest river in the world. Strel swam for ten hours a day and took 66 days to complete his trip. He's been nicknamed "Daredevil," "Fishman," and "The Craziest Man in the World."

The first swimmer to reach the shore was the winner. At first, only men were allowed to compete. Women started to compete in 1912. Most swimming races take place in swimming pools. The swimmers compete in different swimming styles over different distances. However, some swimming competitions still take place in open water, such as rivers, lakes, and the open ocean.

Swim science

Science plays a big role as swimming becomes more competitive. High-tech body suits help to lower drag force as swimmers glide through the water.

Energy gels and sports drinks help to fuel swimmers' bodies. Scientists and coaches study swimmers' techniques with video cameras and **wind tunnels** to help them swim faster. These are just some examples of how science has changed the sport of swimming.

Some races take place in oceans. Swimmers follow a course marked by buoys.

Wind tunnel: A chamber used to study how fluids flow over different objects.

Pool Science

There is more to a swimming pool than just a hole in the ground. In fact, a lot of science goes into designing and maintaining a swimming pool. Competitive swimming takes place in an Olympic-size pool.

Swimming pools are divided into lanes for competitive races.

Olympic pools follow size rules. They must be 82 feet (25 m) wide, 164 feet (50 m) long, and 6.5 feet (two m) deep. The walls of the pool must be strong enough to take the pressure of 5.3 million pints (2.5 million liters) of water. Modern pools are designed to help swimmers. Specially designed lane markers reduce **turbulence**. Pool gutters absorb waves. With many swimmers a day, the water needs to be kept clean and free of germs.

Cleaning with chlorine

Chlorine is a cheap and easy way to keep the water in a pool clean. The chlorine splits into two chemicals when it dissolves in water. Hypochlorous acid kills bacteria quickly. Hypochlorite ions kill bacteria slowly.

 **NEW WORDS**

Turbulence: The irregular flow of water.

Regularly cleaning the pool removes sources of organic nitrogen, such as skin cells.

LOOK CLOSER

What's that smell?

Swimmers leave skin cells, mucus, and dirt in the pool. These are sources of nitrogen. Chlorine reacts with nitrogen to keep the water clean. This happens in a chemical cycle. If there is not enough chlorine, the cycle can stop in the **trichloramine** stage. Trichloramines are what most people think of as the smell in the pool. Adding more chlorine to complete the chemical cycle gets rid of the smell.

It also fades the color from swimsuits. That's why it is important to rinse suits under water after a dip in a chlorinated pool. Some people think that the strong smell in a pool means that too much chlorine has been added to the water. In fact, not enough chlorine causes the smell.

San Alfonso del Mar in Chile is home to the world's largest swimming pool.

▶ ▶ ▶ ▶ ▶ ▶ ▶ ▶

FACT!

Chile pool

The world's biggest swimming pool can be found at a holiday resort in San Alfonso del Mar, Chile. It is two-thirds of a mile (one km) long — that's almost as long as eleven football fields. It holds about 6,000 times more water than an Olympic-size pool.

Trichloramine: A chemical that is produced when chlorine reacts with nitrogen.

Swimming Gear

Swimming gear is pretty simple. The essential items are a swimsuit and a towel—what could be easier?

Other basic equipment includes a swim cap to keep hair out of the water. Some swimmers also use goggles, earplugs, or nose plugs to keep water out of their eyes, ears, and nose.

Training gear

Swimmers use a range of training gear to improve and get faster. They keep track of swim times, both in training and in competition, using stopwatches. Flutter boards, floats, and pull buoys help to improve stroke technique and kicking strength. Swimmers use weights and other gym equipment to strengthen and stretch their muscles.

Most swimmers wear goggles to protect their eyes and a swim cap to keep their hair dry.

NEW WORDS

Drag: The slowing force on a swimmer as he or she moves through the water.

Swimmers use a range of training aids in the pool.

▶▶▶▶▶▶▶▶

FACT!

Record breakers

Many world records have been broken in recent years by swimmers wearing new high-tech swimsuits. Some critics say that the suits give swimmers an unfair lead. They argue that it is similar to allowing fins while racing.

High-tech swimming

As swimming gets more competitive, the gear is getting more high-tech. Scientists have turned to swimsuit technology to help swimmers get faster. Swimmers are constantly fighting against the forces of the water. Some shave their entire bodies to help them slip through the water with less **drag**. New swimsuits are designed to reduce drag. Others help improve muscle performance.

Speedo's Fastskin suit has tiny V-shaped ridges to reduce drag.

LOOK CLOSER

Skinsuits

Speedo's Fastskin suit mimics shark skin. The **hydrodynamic** design of the suit reduces drag. The Adidas Fullbody suit compresses muscles to keep them from getting tired. Arena's Powerskin suit is made of a water-repellent material. Less water gets absorbed in the suit, which makes it lighter. The new Speedo LZR Racer swimsuit is out of this world. Researchers used a NASA wind tunnel, as well as 400 body scans of athletes, to help develop the suit.

Hydrodynamic: The flow of water around an object.

Food for Fuel

Swim training and competitive races use up a lot of energy. Swimmers use muscles in their arms, legs, and torsos. Swimming also takes a lot of concentration to maintain stroke technique and breathing and time perfect turns.

It is important to drink lots of fluid during training.

The body's muscles and brain need a steady supply of energy to work at peak performance. Swimmers must fuel their bodies with a healthy balance of **carbohydrates**, protein, fats, vitamins, and minerals. All these nutrients are found in different foods and drinks.

Food for thought

Cereal grains and fresh fruits and vegetables are good sources of carbohydrates. They provide quick energy for explosive starts and sprint finishes. Protein comes from eggs, lean meats, and nuts. It helps to build and repair muscles. Fats from oils store energy.

NEW WORDS

Carbohydrates: Substances in food made from carbon, hydrogen, and oxygen.

← **Long-distance swimmers need to eat to boost energy supplies.**

This store of body fuel is good for long races. To pack in fast calories between meals, some swimmers turn to energy bars or gels. These quick sources of energy are made up of complex carbohydrates, protein, vitamins, and minerals.

Take a drink

Swimmers sweat just like any athlete. Even though they are surrounded by water, they can become dehydrated. Water will quench thirst, but sports drinks are a better choice. These drinks are specially made to replace lost fluids and **electrolytes** in the body.

FACT!

▶▶▶▶▶▶▶▶

Calorie calculator

Competitive swimmers can use up to 5,000 calories during workouts. An average-size man needs about 2,500 calories a day for regular activity.

▼ **Swimmers should eat a range of different foods to stay healthy.**

LOOK CLOSER

Calorie count

Carbohydrates, fats, and protein are broken down in the body. They react with oxygen to release energy. This energy is measured in calories. One gram of protein or carbohydrate has four calories. One gram of fat has nine calories. A takeout hamburger has up to 700 calories—enough energy to swim for one hour.

Electrolyte: Salt is an example of an electrolyte. It breaks up into charged ions when it dissolves in water.

Water Forces

Swimmers work with and against the forces of the water each time they train or compete.

Buoyancy is the upward force of water on a swimmer's body. This force helps to keep swimmers afloat. An opposite, downward force of **gravity** pulls a swimmer down. Gravity is caused by the pull of the Earth on objects. Buoyancy and gravity work against each other. If the force of buoyancy is greater than the force of gravity, a swimmer will float.

Drag slows a swimmer down. Water is 700 times more dense than air and provides more resistance. That's why wading knee deep in water is much harder than walking on the beach.

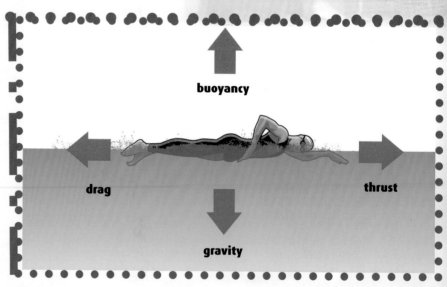

There are four forces at work when you swim at the surface of the water.

buoyancy

drag

thrust

gravity

NEW WORDS

Gravity: Force that pulls things toward the center of the Earth.

12

Fighting forces

Gravity acts through the body's center of gravity, which usually lies between the swimmer's hips and belly button. The lower part of the body is denser (bones and muscles of the legs) than the top half (lungs, arms, and head). The center of buoyancy is usually a bit higher.

LOOK CLOSER

Floating facts

A swimmer will float depending on where the center of gravity and center of buoyancy are on his or her body. The center of buoyancy and the center of gravity are closer together in children. So the body of a child stays flatter in the water and floating is easier.

It is the average position of the buoyant force acting on the body. As swimmers float, gravity pulls down through the center of gravity. Buoyancy forces push up through the center of buoyancy. So the lower part of the body hangs down in the water, while the upper body stays afloat.

The same four forces are acting on this swimmer as she stretches out under the water.

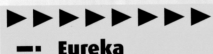

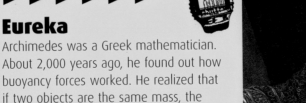
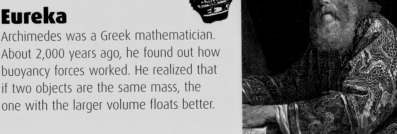

FACT!

Eureka

Archimedes was a Greek mathematician. About 2,000 years ago, he found out how buoyancy forces worked. He realized that if two objects are the same mass, the one with the larger volume floats better.

Buoyancy: The upward force of the water that pushes on a swimmer in the pool.

Cutting through the Water

A swimmer swims from start to finish as quickly as possible. He or she aims for maximum propulsion and minimum drag.

Swimmers can improve their speed in a few ways. Strong, powerful muscles in the arms, legs, and torso aid propulsion. But a lot of this power is wasted if the swimmer has poor stroke technique.

Reducing drag

All moving objects experience drag force as they move through air or water. Water is denser than air, so a swimmer needs to work harder to overcome the resistance of the water. Swimmers can reduce drag when diving in the pool or pushing off the wall by **streamlining**. This means holding the body flat and long, with the arms in front and legs tucked together.

↑ *A swimmer stretches his body to stay streamlined. This helps to cut down drag.*

NEW WORDS

Molecule: The smallest particle of a chemical compound, which is made up of two or more atoms.

Efficient stroke technique is the key to fast swimming.

Kicking the legs keeps them in line with the rest of the body. An angled hand position during the stroke helps to produce lift. Stretching with each stroke keeps the body streamlined. All these techniques help to reduce the force of drag.

A swimmer catches his breath in the bow wave created by his head.

LOOK CLOSER

Different types of drag

Frictional drag: Water **molecules** absorb energy as they bounce off the swimmer's body. This drag is like the resistance you feel when you rub your hand against sand paper.

Pressure drag: Water builds up in front of the swimmer as he or she speeds through the water. High pressure builds up at the head. The pressure at the feet is lower. The pressure difference causes a sucking force at the feet.

Wave drag: Swimming creates waves around the body. At a certain speed, the wave length is equal to the length of the swimmer's body. This wave drag slows down the swimmer. If the swimmer tries to swim out of the pocket, wave drag gets worse. This limits the top speed a swimmer can reach.

Streamlining: Making the body flat and long to cut through the water with minimum drag.

Fit to Swim

Like all athletes, swimmers need to warm up and stretch before training sessions or races.

A ten-minute warm-up of easy swimming boosts blood flow to the muscles. After the warm-up, stretching the shoulders, back, chest, legs, and arms reduces the risk of injuries. Each stretch should be done two or three times and held for between 15 and 30 seconds.

⬆ *It is important to warm up before an important race.*

FACT!

▶▶▶▶▶▶▶▶

Ian Thorpe

Ian Thorpe is an Australian Olympic Gold medal swimmer. Thorpe trained 35 hours a week to get his body in shape. He swam up to 75 miles (120 km) each week.

Sets and drills

Swimmers run through a series of drills to perfect stroke technique. Each drill focuses on one part of the stroke at a time. An example is a front crawl drill called "catch-up." Swimmers do only arm pulls during the drill.

NEW WORDS

Cross training: Keeping fit by training in sports other than swimming.

Stretching keeps the muscles supple and ready for competition.

LOOK CLOSER

Cross training

Swimmers do more than just swim to keep in top shape. **Cross training** helps to build a strong, balanced body. This helps prevent injuries. Strength training in the gym helps tone muscles that might not be used regularly in swimming. Running helps build **endurance** for long swim races. Cross training is also a great way to keep training interesting.

They concentrate on one side of the body at a time. By repeating the movement over and over, the muscles "remember" the swimming movements until it becomes automatic. A series of drills focusing on different parts of the stroke is called a set. Sets help swimmers perfect their stroke technique and swim stronger.

Brain training

A swimmer's brain must also be ready for the race. Competitive swimmers use visualization to help them perform to their best abilities. They prepare their minds by thinking through starts, turns, and stroke rate. Running through the race, step-by-step, helps to focus the mind better on race day.

Swimming aids, such as paddles, help to improve stroke technique.

Endurance: A measure of an athlete's ability to keep on exercising.

Stroke Science Crawl

The front crawl, or freestyle, is the most common swimming stroke. It is also the fastest. Each part of the stroke and kick is to drive the swimmer forward and overcome the forces of drag.

During the pull, the hand pulls water from the front to the back of the body. Originally, swimmers brought the hand straight back through the water during the pull. But this technique wastes a lot of energy and creates drag.

The propulsion **of the crawl comes from the arms. One arm pulls while the other recovers.**

NEW WORDS

Propulsion: The force that drives a swimmer forward. Propulsion is created by the swimmer's arms and legs.

FACT! Record breaker

In 2007, American swimmer Kate Ziegler shaved more than nine seconds off the 0.9-mile (1,500-m) freestyle world record, with a time of 15 minutes and 42 seconds.

A more efficient pull uses an angled hand through the water. Also, using an S-type movement, called **sculling**, lets the hand come in contact with more water. This increases the power of the pull.

Recovery

While one arm is pulling, the other is recovering and preparing for the next stroke. Extending the hand as much as possible with each stroke lengthens the body and reduces wave drag.

Breathing

The swimmer takes a breath every two or three strokes. Sighting the bottom of the pool between breaths ensures the swimmer is going in a straight line.

The kick

The flutter kick helps to balance the body in the water. The legs kick to help keep the body flat and reduce drag. The kick also provides some propulsive forces, but not as much as the arm pulls.

Sculling: Moving the hands in a S-shape through the water to increase the power of the pull.

Stroke Science Breaststroke

The breaststroke is one of the slowest swimming strokes. But that does not mean it is the easiest. It takes a lot of practice to time the arm pull, whip kick, and breathing into one fluid stroke.

The breaststroke is done on the front. To start, the palms are together at the chest. The legs are straight and together. The legs then whip kick similar to the way in which a frog kicks. This forces the body forward. The arms reach to the front in a glide as the legs come back together. The arms then pull the water back. The hands are tilted at an angle and move in an outward, then inward, sculling motion. The palms come back together at the chest. The face comes out of the water to take a breath. This completes one cycle of the stroke.

➡ *Swimmers need to work on their technique to master the breaststroke.*

NEW WORDS

Tumble turns: Flip turns used to change directions when approaching the wall of the pool.

LOOK CLOSER

Kicking power

In the breaststroke, the swimmer gets most power from the whip kick. The arm stroke drives the body forward, too, but its main job is to let the swimmer take a breath and get the body back into position for the next kick.

The whip kick provides about 70 percent of the breaststroke's power.

Breaststroke rules

Freestyle and butterfly swimmers do **tumble turns** to change directions at the end of the lane. Breaststroke swimmers do "open turns." They touch the wall with both hands and rotate to push off with their feet. Swimmers must be belly down as they push off. They are allowed one **dolphin kick** while streamlining before their first stroke. When finishing the race, they must also touch the wall with both hands.

▶ ▶ ▶ ▶ ▶ ▶ ▶ ▶

FACT!

Liesel Jones

Australian Liesel Jones (pictured left) was 15 when she took silver in the 333-feet (100-m) breaststroke at the 2000 Sydney Olympics. This made her the youngest ever Olympic swimming medallist.

Dolphin kick: An undulating kick in which the legs are held together and move up and down.

Stroke Science
Backstroke

As its name suggests, the backstroke, or back crawl, is swum on the back. The arms take turns pulling water, while the legs flutter kick to aid propulsion.

At the start and at turns, backstroke swimmers glide under the water.

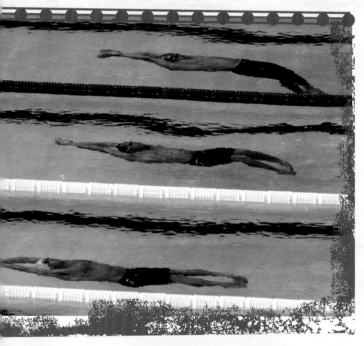

To start the backstroke, one hand comes out of the water, thumb first, near the hip. The shoulder and hip rotate up as the arm windmills and reaches above the head. The hand then enters the water above the head, smallest finger first, to start the underwater pull. The arm draws through the water in a sculling motion, similar to a backward front crawl. While one arm is pulling, the other is recovering.

Body rotation

Rotating the body with each stroke helps in two ways. First, when the body slices through the water on an angle, similar to the V-shape of the bottom of a boat, there is less resistance. Second, tilting the body lets the large torso muscles add power to the stroke.

NEW WORDS

Flutter kick: The most common swimming kick in which the legs move up and down without bending the knees.

Kicking

The **flutter kick** is similar to the one used in front crawl, but it is upside down. It adds a bit of propulsion, but its main job is to keep the legs and body in a straight, streamlined position. This reduces drag.

▶ ▶ ▶ ▶ ▶ ▶ ▶ ▶

FACT!

Natalie Coughlin

American Natalie Coughlin became the first ever woman to break the one minute barrier in the 333-ft (100-meter) backstroke in 2002. She broke her own World Record in 2007 when she swam it in 59.44 seconds.

⬇ *The arm you can see above the water is in the recovery phase of the stroke.*

LOOK CLOSER

Poor technique

Overreaching, leading the stroke with the back of the hand, and entering too wide are common backstroke mistakes. These poor techniques all add drag and slow the swimmer down.

⬆ *To keep the head perfectly still, this backstroke swimmer is balancing a bottle on her head while swimming.*

Backstroke markers

During the backstroke, the head is kept still with the chin tucked in. Flags across the pool show the swimmer that there are only 16 feet (five m) left before the wall. That way, the swimmer can prepare for the next turn or a sprint to the finish.

Overreaching: When a swimmer reaches too far with his or her hand during the stroke.

Stroke Science
Butterfly

The butterfly is the hardest swimming stroke to master. It takes a lot of practice to combine the arm pull, dolphin kick, and breathing into a smooth, gliding stroke.

The swimmer starts the stroke in a glide position. The body is straight, with the arms outstretched in front of the body. The face is in the water. To start the first pull, the swimmer bends the legs up at the knee and kicks them both together like a dolphin's tail. Both arms pull through the water to drive the body forward. The pull is similar to the crawl, but both arms pull together.

Stroke sequence

During the recovery phase, the swimmer kicks again to lift the head, arms, and upper chest out of the water. The swimmer usually takes a breath every other stroke.

⬆ *As with all swimming strokes, the swimmer breathes in during the recovery and breathes out under the water.*

NEW WORDS ● ● ● ● ● ● ● ● ● ● ● ● ● ●

Peak speed: The fastest part of a swimming stroke.

24

FACT!

▶ ▶ ▶ ▶ ▶ ▶ ▶ ▶

Michael Phelps

American Michael Phelps (pictured right) has broken the 666-ft (200-m) butterfly World Record six times. He broke his own record at the 2008 Beijing Olympics, where he won eight gold medals in different events.

The hands then enter the water, thumbs first and shoulder width apart, and the swimmer dives forward into the water. A small whip kick keeps the legs from sinking too far down into the water before the next stroke.

Stroke speed

The **peak speed** of the butterfly is quicker than the front crawl, because both arms pull together. It is slower overall, however, because the stroke slows down during the **recovery phase**.

➡ *The butterfly is similar to the front crawl, but both arms pull and recover at the same time.*

LOOK CLOSER

Building the butterfly

Swimming coach David Armbruster invented the butterfly in 1934. He wanted to develop a stroke that would reduce drag and improve the speed of the breaststroke. Armbruster found that by bringing the arms out of the water, swimmers moved faster. One of his swimmers, Jack Sieg, came up with the dolphin kick a year later. They put the stroke and the kick together to create the butterfly.

Recovery phase: The part of the stroke when the swimmer gets ready for the next power phase.

Racing Tactics

Modern Olympic races have 32 events for swimmers. Pool races range from 160 to 4,800 ft (50 to 1,500 meters). There is also a 6¼-mile (10-km) open-water race.

Swim races are won and lost in hundredths of a second. An explosive start is vital. At the first starter's signal, the swimmers take position on the **starting blocks** (or backstroke grips). Their hands reach down to the blocks, one on top of the other.

All the races apart from backstroke start from the starting blocks.

➡️ *A swimmer tumble turns at the end of the lane and drives off the wall to start the next length.*

The swimmers tuck their heads in and curl their toes over the edges of the blocks to help push off.The knees are bent, ready to dive forward when the starting pistol fires. The swimmers then dive into the water and stretch out into a streamlined position to prevent drag.

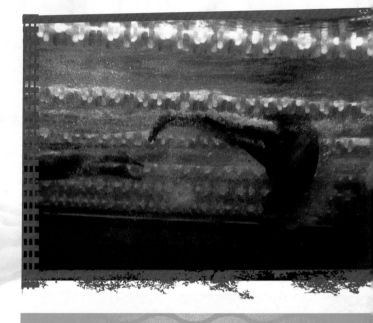

Tumble turns

A tumble turn is a quick, efficient way for a swimmer to change direction at the end of the lane. A compact tuck and streamlined body after the push off helps to reduce drag. It is important for swimmers to stay strong through the middle of the race. If a swimmer does not stay focused, this is where valuable time can be lost.

LOOK CLOSER

Race for the clock

Swimmers tag an electronic touch pad set at the end of each lane when they finish. Touching the pad sends a signal to the timing clock. The finish time is then registered on the scoreboard.

▶▶▶▶▶▶▶▶

FACT!

Mark Spitz

At the 1972 Olympics, Mark Spitz won seven gold medals. His record lasted until 2008, when Michael Phelps took eight golds. The International Olympic Committee (IOC) chose Spitz as one of its five athletes of the century. Phelps is sure to follow.

NEW WORDS

Starting blocks: Raised platforms on which the swimmers wait for the race to start (apart from backstroke races).

The Future of Swimming

Swimmers, scientists, and personal trainers continue to find new ways to improve pool technology and swimming times. New ideas are sure to keep this exciting sport on the cutting edge of science for years to come.

An endless pool is a miniature version of a normal swimming pool. Swimmers swim against a current in a similar way to a runner moving over the escalator of a treadmill. The pool can be kept so small because the swimmer does not really move. The speed of the current can be adjusted to suit the swimmer. An endless pool can move up to 40,000 pints (19,000 liters) of water a minute.

Sports scientists use an endless pool to assess the fitness of a swimmer.

NEW WORDS

Nanotechnology: Technology that involves working with substances at the molecular level.

Swimming in miniature

Nanotechnology is the science of changing matter on an atomic or molecular level. One company is using nanotechnology to treat pool water. Their device uses **crystals** that convert bacteria, skin cells, and other organic waste into carbon dioxide and water. The waste is broken down into simple molecules so there are no solids to be filtered from the pool.

Pool technology

Many pools are now fitted with electronic control systems. A computer monitors the pool water and pumps. If there is a problem, the system adjusts the pool settings automatically. As a result, the owner does not have to spend as much time looking after the pool.

Coaches video swimmers to assess stroke technique.

Computational fluid dynamics is used to map the flow of water around a swimmer's body.

LOOK CLOSER

Computational fluid dynamics (CFD)

CFD uses math to model and predict the flow of fluids such as water. CFD has been used in the oil industry for years. Sports scientists and coaches are now using it to help train their athletes. An Australian research project is looking for ways to use CFD to help their Olympic swimmers. By studying how water flows past swimmers, coaches can help to find new ways to overcome drag and increase swimming power.

Crystals: Solids made of atoms, molecules, or ions that are held together in a regular, repeating pattern.

Glossary

buoyancy The upward force of the water that pushes on a swimmer in the pool

carbohydrates Substances in food made from carbon, hydrogen, and oxygen

cross training Keeping fit by training in sports other than swimming

crystals Solids consisting of atoms, molecules, or ions that are held together in a regular, repeating pattern

dolphin kick An undulating kick in which the legs are held together and move up and down

drag The slowing force on a swimmer as he or she moves through the water

electrolyte Salt is an example of an electrolyte. It breaks up into charged ions when it dissolves in water

endurance A measure of an athlete's ability to keep on exercising

FINA The Fédération Internationale de Natation is the world governing body for swimming competitions

flutter kick The most common swimming kick in which the legs move up and down without bending the knees

gravity Force that pulls things toward the center of the Earth

hydrodynamic The flow of water around an object

molecule The smallest particle of a chemical compound, which is made up of two or more atoms

nanotechnology Technology that involves working with substances at the molecular level

overreaching When a swimmer reaches too far with his or her hand during the stroke

peak speed The fastest part of a swimming stroke

propulsion The force that drives a swimmer forward. Propulsion is created by the swimmer's arms and legs

recovery phase The part of the stroke when the swimmer gets ready for the next power phase

sculling Moving the hands in a S-shape through the water to increase the power of the pull

starting blocks Raised platforms on which the swimmers wait for the race to start (apart from backstroke races)

streamlining Making the body flat and long to cut through the water with minimum drag

trichloramine A chemical that is produced when chlorine reacts with nitrogen

tumble turns Flip turns used to change directions when approaching the wall of the pool

turbulence The irregular flow of water

wind tunnel A chamber used to study how fluids flow over different objects

Find Out More

Books

Crossingham, John, Niki Walker, and Bonna Rouse. *Swimming in Action (Sports in Action)*. New York: Crabtree Publishing Company, 2003.

Fridell, Ron. *Sports Technology (Cool Science)*. Minneapolis, Minnesota: Lerner Publications, 2008.

Gifford, Clive. *Swimming (Personal Best)*. New York: PowerKids Press, 2008.

Mason, Paul. *How to Improve at Swimming*. New York: Crabtree Publishing Company, 2008.

Timblin, Stephen. *Swimming (21st Century Skills Innovation Library)*. North Mankato, Minnesota: Cherry Lake Publishing, 2008.

Wiese, Jim, and Ed Shems. *Sports Science: 40 Goal-Scoring, High-Flying, Medal-Winning Experiments for Kids*. New York: Wiley, 2002.

Websites

The About.com website explains everything you need to know about swimming. Click on links such as "Psychology & Swim Science" and "Swimming Technique Tips" to find out more detailed information on swimming science and stroke technique.

swimming.about.com

This website explores the physics behind swimming — everything from Archimedes' principle to Newton's laws of motion.

www.east-buc.k12.ia.us/02_03/CE/km/TP.htm

This self-help guide aims to help nervous swimmers relax in the water. Click on the "Physics" link to find out more about swimming science.

www.relaxnswim.com/index.html

Index

Printed in the U.S.A. – BG